Encounters with God

The First and Second Epistles of Paul the Apostle to the THESSALONIANS

Encounters with God Study Guide Series

The Gospel of Matthew

The Gospel of Mark

The Gospel of Luke

The Gospel of John

The Book of Acts

The Book of Romans

The First Epistle of Paul the Apostle to the Corinthians

The Second Epistle of Paul the Apostle to the Corinthians

The Epistle of Paul the Apostle to the Galatians

The Epistle of Paul the Apostle to the Ephesians

The Epistle of Paul the Apostle to the Philippians

The Epistles of Paul the Apostle to the Colossians and Philemon

The First and Second Epistles of Paul the Apostle to the Thessalonians

The First and Second Epistles of Paul the Apostle to Timothy and Titus

The Epistle of Paul the Apostle to the Hebrews

The Epistle of James

The First and Second Epistles of Peter

The First, Second, and Third Epistles of John and Jude

The Revelation of Jesus Christ

Encounters with God

The First and Second Epistles of Paul the Apostle to the THESSALONIANS

Published in Nashville, Tennessee, by Thomas Nelson. Thomas Nelson is a registered trademark of Thomas Nelson, Inc.

Thomas Nelson, Inc. titles may be purchased in bulk for educational, business, fund-raising, or sales promotional use. For information, please e-mail SpecialMarkets@ThomasNelson.com.

ISBN 978-1-4185-2650-4

Printed in the United States of America

08 09 10 11 12 RRD 5 4 3 2 1

CONTENTS

AN INTRODUCTION TO THE FIRST AND SECOND EPISTLES TO THE THESSALONIANS

This study guide covers two epistles from the apostle Paul to the first-century church that Paul and his evangelistic traveling companions had established at Thessalonica, Greece. Both are fairly short letters written to the Thessalonians in the middle of the first century, only two decades after Jesus' death and resurrection. The first letter to the Thessalonians is one of the earliest of Paul's canonical letters. The second letter appears to have been written about six months after the first letter.

The apostle Paul, accompanied by his colleagues Silas and Timothy, went to Thessalonica on Paul's first missionary journey. Paul arrived in Thessalonica from Philippi, where he and Silas had been imprisoned after Paul spoke words of deliverance to a slave girl possessed with a spirit of divination. Paul and Silas were miraculously released from prison and, after receiving a public apology from the Philippian magistrates and then meeting with new believers in Lydia's house, they departed Philippi. They passed through Amphipolis and Apollonia to arrive in Thessalonica. There, they went to a Jewish synagogue and reasoned from the Scriptures for three Sabbaths "explaining and demonstrating that the Christ had to suffer and rise again from the dead." Paul boldly proclaimed, "This Jesus whom I preach to you is the Christ." The book of Acts says some of the Jews were persuaded to accept Jesus as the Christ, along with a great multitude of devout Greeks that included a number of leading women in the city (Acts 17:1–4).

The Jews of Thessalonica retaliated against Paul's message and created a riotous scene before the rulers of the city. The city's new Christians were able to gain Paul and Silas' release from the city rulers. When the Thessalonian Jews caused trouble in Berea, Paul was sent on to Athens. Silas and Timothy remained in Berea for a short while and then rejoined Paul.

While Paul was in Corinth on his second missionary journey, he received a report from Timothy, who had just returned from the church in Thessalonica. Paul wrote to the Thessalonians from Corinth to express his general thanksgiving and satisfaction with their lives as new believers, to answer charges that were brought against him by some Jewish opponents, to encourage believers in the faith, and to correct misconceptions they appeared to have about the second coming of Christ.

Thessalonica was the capital of Macedonia and its largest city. It was located on the Via Egnatia, the main Roman highway to the east. This location gave the believers in Thessalonica a significant opportunity to help spread the gospel message toward the eastern provinces of the Roman Empire.

Thessalonica was basically Greek, but it had a strong Jewish community. Those who came to Christ from the Greek population likely had been pagan idolaters who became God-fearing Greeks. The church was a blend of Jewish and Gentile believers, and based on Paul's letters, it appears the two groups mixed well in the new church. Strong statements are made in both letters to the Thessalonians applauding the love that flowed freely in this new church.

The second letter to the Thessalonians is just a continuation. Paul appears to have still been in Corinth, penning a second letter that clarifies some of the first letter. It also provided a strong follow-up word of encouragement to continue to live steadfastly in the faith.

About the Author, the Apostle Paul. The author of these letters to the Thessalonians is the apostle Paul. He identifies himself as the author (1 Thess. 1:1, 2:18; 2 Thess. 1:1), and the early church acknowledged his authorship. Some have questioned whether Paul wrote the second letter to the Thessalonians since this letter has a few phrases and words not common to the rest of Paul's writings. The letter itself, however, states that Paul is the author. In many cases men such as Paul dictated their letters to scribes who served as executive secretaries. Those who actually took down the words often took some liberty when it came to phraseology and vocabulary. Overall, though, the message of 2 Thessalonians totally keeps with Paul's theology, his concerns as an evangelist and apostle, and his practical preaching to other churches that he established.

Paul's name was originally Saul (Acts 13:9), the royal name of Israel's first king. Upon his conversion, he adopted the name Paul, which literally meant "little" and reflected his self-evaluation as being "the least of the apostles" (1 Cor. 15:9). In the history of Christianity, the "little" apostle became the foremost apostle to the Gentile world.

Paul was a Roman citizen from Tarsus, the chief city of Cilicia. He was fluent in Greek, studied philosophy and theology under Gamaliel, and was also a Hebrew, the son of a Pharisee from the tribe of Benjamin. Paul, too, became a Pharisee, a very strict follower of Jewish religious laws. By trade, he was a tentmaker. This unique blend of cultural, religious, and experiential factors gave Paul unusual entrée into both Gentile and Jewish circles.

Initially, Paul was a major force in denouncing Christianity in Jerusalem and a willing witness to Stephen's martyrdom. While on a mission to seek out and destroy Christians who had traveled to Syria, Paul had a dramatic encounter with the risen Christ. In the aftermath he became just as zealous a believer in Christ Jesus and advocate for the gospel as he once had been a zealous foe to the early church. He took several fruitful and demanding missionary journeys, spending as long as two years in some areas to teach those who had heeded the gospel message and accepted Jesus as their Savior. Over the decades of his ministry, he became the most influential church planter and theologian in the early church. His letters addressed both the triumphs and difficulties encountered by the first-century Christians, many of whom faced intense persecution for their faith.

The issues Paul addressed in his letters to the first-century church are no less important to today's believers. Paul laid a very practical foundation for how to live the Christian life, even in the face of struggles, temptations, and heresies. His personal example of seeking to know and obey Christ Jesus no matter the cost remains an example to all who call themselves Christians. "I in Christ and Christ in me" was Paul's unwavering theme song.

AN OVERVIEW OF OUR STUDY OF THE FIRST AND SECOND EPISTLES TO THE THESSALONIANS

This study guide presents seven lessons drawn from the epistles of 1 and 2 Thessalonians. It elaborates upon the commentary included in the *Blackaby Study Bible*:

Lesson #1: Faithful and Exemplary Believers

Lesson #2: Fruitful and Truthful Ministers

Lesson #3: Overcoming Satan's Hindrances

Lesson #4: Abounding More and More

Lesson #5: Ready for Christ's Coming

Lesson #6: Resistance to Apostasy

Lesson #7: Admonitions and Blessings

Personal or Group Use. These lessons are offered for personal study and reflection or for small-group Bible study. The study questions asked may be answered by an individual reader or used as a foundation for group discussion. A segment titled "Notes to Leaders of Small Groups" is included at the back of this book to help those leading a group study of this material.

Before you embark on this study, we encourage you to read in full the statement in the *Blackaby Study Bible* titled "How to Study the Bible." Our contention is always that the Bible is unique among all literature. It is God's definitive word for humanity. The Bible is

- *inspired*—"God-breathed"

- *authoritative*—absolutely the final word on any spiritual matter

- *the plumb line of truth*—the standard against which all human activity and reasoning must be evaluated

The Bible is fascinating in that it has remarkable diversity but also remarkable unity. Its books were penned by a diverse assortment of authors representing a variety of languages and cultures, and it contains a number of literary forms. But the Bible's message from cover to cover is clear, consistent, and unified.

More than mere words on a page, the Bible is an encounter with God Himself. No book is more critical to your life. The very essence of the Bible is the Lord Himself.

The Holy Spirit speaks through the Bible. He also communicates during your time of prayer, in your life circumstances, and through the church. Read your Bible in an attitude of prayer, and allow the Holy Spirit to make you aware of God's activity in and through your personal life. Write down what you learn, meditate on it, and adjust your thoughts, attitudes, and behavior accordingly. Look for ways every day to apply the truth of God's Word to your circumstances and relationships. God is not random; He is orderly and intentional in the way He speaks to you.

Be encouraged—the Bible is *not* too difficult for the average person to understand if that person asks the Holy Spirit for help. (Furthermore, not even the most brilliant person can fully understand the Bible apart from the Holy Spirit's help.) God desires for you to know Him and to know His Word. Every person who reads the Bible can learn from it. The person who will receive *maximum* benefits from reading and studying the Bible, however, is the person who:

- *is born again* (John 3:3,5). Those who are born again and have received the gift of His Spirit have a distinct advantage in understanding the deeper truths of God's Word.

- *has a heart that desires to learn God's truth.* Your attitude greatly influences the outcome of Bible study. Resist the temptation to focus on what others have said about the Bible. Allow the Holy Spirit to guide you as you study God's Word for yourself.

- *has a heart that seeks to obey God.* The Holy Spirit teaches the most to those who desire to apply what they learn.

Begin your Bible study with prayer, asking the Holy Spirit to guide your thoughts and to impress upon you what is on God's heart. Then make plans to adjust your life immediately to obey the Lord fully.

As you read and study the Bible, your purpose is not to *create* meaning, but to *discover* the meaning of the text with the Holy Spirit's guidance. Ask yourself, "What did the author have in mind? How was this applied by those who first heard these words?" Especially in your study of Paul's letters, look for ways in which the truths can be applied directly to your personal, practical, daily Christian walk and to the life of your church.

At times you may find it helpful to consult other passages of the Bible (made available in the center columns in the *Blackaby Study Bible*), or the commentary that is in the margins of the *Blackaby Study Bible*.

Keep in mind always that Bible study is not primarily an exercise for acquiring information but an opportunity for transformation. Bible study is your opportunity to encounter God and to be changed in His presence. When God speaks to your heart, nothing remains the same. Jesus said, "He who has ears to hear, let him hear" (Matt. 13:9). Choose to have ears that desire to hear.

The B-A-S-I-Cs of Each Study in This Guide. Each lesson in this study guide has five segments, using the word BASIC as an acronym. The word BASIC does not allude to elementary or simple, but rather to foundational. These studies extend the concepts that are part of the *Blackaby Study Bible* commentary and are focused on key aspects of what it means to be a Christ-follower in today's world. The BASIC acronym stands for:

B = *Bible Focus*. This segment presents the central passage for the lesson and a general explanation that covers the central theme or concern.

A = *Application for Today*. This segment has a story or illustration related to current-day events with questions that link the Bible text to today's issues, problems, and concerns.

S = *Supplementary Scriptures to Consider*. In this segment other Bible verses related to the general theme of the lesson are explored.

I = *Introspection and Implications*. In this segment questions are asked that lead to deeper reflection about one's personal faith journey and life experiences.

C = *Communicating the Good News*. In this segment challenging questions point to ways the lesson's truth might be lived out and shared with others, whether to win the lost or build up the church.

LESSON #1

FAITHFUL AND EXEMPLARY BELIEVERS

*Exemplary: something so good or admirable
that others would do well to copy it*

B
Bible Focus

> *You became followers of us and of the Lord, having re-*
> *ceived the word in much affliction, with joy of the Holy Spirit,*
> *so that you became examples to all in Macedonia and Achaia*
> *who believe. For from you the word of the Lord has sounded*
> *forth, not only in Macedonia and Achaia, but also in every*
> *place. Your faith toward God has gone out, so that we do not*
> *need to say anything.*
>
> *For they themselves declare concerning us what manner of*
> *entry we had to you, and how you turned to God from idols to*
> *serve the living and true God, and to wait for his Son from*
> *heaven, whom He raised from the dead, even Jesus who*
> *delivers us from the wrath to come . . .*
>
> *For this reason we also thank God without ceasing, because*
> *when you received the word of God which you heard from us,*
> *you welcomed it not as the word of men, but as it is in truth,*
> *the word of God, which also effectively works in you who*
> *believe.*
>
> *For you, brethren, became imitators of the churches of God*
> *which are in Judea in Christ Jesus. For you also suffered the*
> *same things from your own countrymen, just as they did from*
> *the Judeans (1 Thess. 1:6–10, 2:13–14).*

The Thessalonian church was a fairly new church, hardly a few years old when Paul wrote them. Paul established the church during a fairly brief visit that he, Silvanus (Silas), and Timothy made to the city of Thessalonica. It doesn't appear that Paul was in Thessalonica for more than a few weeks. We know from Acts that Paul reasoned from the Scriptures in the Jewish syna-gogue for three weeks, presented Jesus as the Christ, persuading some of the Jews, a large number of devout Greeks, and some of the leading women of the city. Then the Jews who felt threatened by his message instigated a riot against Paul, and he was smuggled out of the city and sent to Berea before going on to Athens. Silas and Timothy remained in Berea for a short period and then followed Paul to Athens.

Perhaps the most telling attribute of this young church was that, though born in controversy and affliction, its believers received the gospel message with "joy of the Holy Spirit" (1 Thess. 1:5–6). They heard the message of Christ preached powerfully and confidently, with accompanying signs and wonders (1 Thess. 1:5). They responded enthusiastically and joyfully to this message. Paul readily recognized in writing to them that it was the Holy Spirit's work in their midst that had allowed them to become such an exemplary church to all in the surrounding regions of Macedonia and Achaia.

In many ways the Holy Spirit became the teacher and guide for this new church. Although Silas and Timothy continued to teach the new believers for a short while after Paul left, the church was eventually left on its own to study the Scriptures and rely upon the Holy Spirit for ongoing direction and counsel. The Thessalonian believers, Paul said, were quick to recognize the "truth, the word of God" and to apply it to their lives. They had not only become the followers of Paul, but followers of the Lord (1 Thess. 1:6, 2:13).

Paul told this church that he loved them as a nursing mother loves her infant—tenderly and completely (1 Thess. 2:7). But he recognized that it was God, their loving heavenly Father, who was strengthening and guiding them. It was the Holy Spirit's work in the church that had allowed its members to

- turn definitively to Christ, leaving behind all idols and sin,

- serve the living God and stand firm, even in times of suffering and affliction, and

- remain strong in faith, patiently waiting for Jesus to return to earth.

Some people argue that a church must have strong, mature leadership in order for new converts and immature Christians to grow strong in the faith. That certainly appears to be true when it comes to *establishing* a church. And, it certainly is the ideal for ongoing leadership. Even so, an ideal model isn't always possible, and it certainly isn't a requirement. Countless "baby" believers have grown strong and mature in the wake of powerful evangelistic campaigns in remote regions of the world. These new converts, and also "baby" churches which grow strong, seem to bear two great characteristics: First, the new converts to Christ heard a biblically sound and convincing presentation of the Gospel, with verifying "power" and "much assurance" (1 Thess. 1:5). Second, the new converts continued to rely upon the Holy Spirit to illuminate Bible truth to them and to shape their lives according to God's divine will.

What an encouraging message these opening statements of Paul should be to those today who proclaim the message of Christ as evangelists. Preach with power, and in much assurance. Those who respond to your message with joy *can* grow in Christ and carry on the banner of the Gospel in an effective and lasting way. They can become effective, exemplary, and faithful followers of Christ Jesus.

A
Application for Today

Consider this scenario: You and two of your friends are dropped off on a small island with the understanding that the ship will be back in a few weeks to pick you up, should you want to leave the island at that time. In the future, the transporting ship might come by the island every three or four months. You have been told that the people on the island have never heard the name of Jesus.

What would be your strategy for presenting the gospel to this unreached people?

What items would you plan to take with you to this island? Which of these items would you plan to leave behind? (Be conservative—limit the items you would take to one large suitcase or duffel bag per person.)

How long would you plan to stay? Why? What would be your exit strategy or the criterion for you to move on?

What would you do if you encountered severe persecution, perhaps even threats of death, from those who saw their positions of leadership being threatened by your message?

What would you build into your plan of evangelism to ensure that the new converts had all they needed to continue to grow in Christ after you left?

Consider this scenario: the "island" to which you are going is an inner-city neighborhood covering one square mile. Now, what would your strategy be? How would you equip yourselves? How long would you plan to stay? Why? What would be your exit strategy?

S
Supplementary Scriptures to Consider

Paul was quick to note that the Word of God, which the Thessalonians had received as the truth of God, was working effectively in them, enabling them to endure harsh persecution:

> We also thank God without ceasing, because when you
> received the word of God which you heard from us, you
> welcomed it not as the word of men, but as it is in truth, the
> word of God, which also effectively works in you who be-
> lieve. For you, brethren, became imitators of the churches of
> God which are in Judea in Christ Jesus. For you also suffered
> the same things from your own countrymen, just as they did
> from the Judeans, who killed both the Lord Jesus and their
> own prophets, and have persecuted us; and they do not please

God and are contrary to all men, forbidding us to speak to the
Gentiles that they may be saved, so as always to fill up the
measure of their sins; but wrath has come upon them to the
uttermost (1 Thess. 2:13–16).

• What is the difference between receiving a sermon message or teaching
   lesson as "the word of men" and receiving it as "the word of God"?

• How can you tell if the word of God is "effectively" working in you as an
   individual? In your church as a whole?

• Do you feel prepared to withstand serious persecution from your country-
   men, which may include your family members, friends, or people in your
   neighborhood and business arena? What might you do to prepare yourself
   more fully? How might that persecution come to you or your church in
   the future?

• What is the difference between being persecuted individually for your faith and having your persecutors put up roadblocks that prohibit you from speaking the gospel message to others?

Jesus taught the importance of abiding in the truth:

> Jesus said to those Jews who believed Him, "If you abide in My word, you are My disciples indeed. And you shall know the truth, and the truth shall make you free" (John 8:31–32).

• How does knowing Jesus translate into knowing the truth? ("Jesus said, 'I am the way, the truth, and the life'" John 14:6).

• In what ways does the truth free us from heretical "words of men"?

I
Introspection and Implications

1. What is the difference between a person who becomes a genuine follower of Jesus Christ and one who becomes a follower of "men only?"

2. What do you believe the apostle Paul would write to *your* church? Would he consider you exemplary and faithful believers?

3. If the apostle Paul wrote to your church, what would his appraisal be regarding:

   a. your definitive turning from sin to follow Christ?

b. your service to the living God in the face of suffering or persecution?

c. your patience in waiting for the return of Christ?

4. Do you have the joy of the Holy Spirit about the gospel you profess to believe? Why or why not?

C
Communicating the Good News

Paul wrote, "Our gospel did not come to you in word only, but also in power, and in the Holy Spirit and in much assurance, as you know what kind of men we were among you for your sake" (1 Thess. 1:5).

How can we present the Gospel in power and not in word only?

How is the Gospel presented "in the Holy Spirit"?

What does it mean to present the Gospel "in much assurance"?

What do you think Paul meant when he said, "you know what kind of men we were among you *for your sake?*" In what ways is a person's personal reputation important to another person's receiving the gospel message? Why?

Lesson #2

FRUITFUL AND TRUTHFUL MINISTERS

*Exhortation: earnestly advising or urging strongly,
either in admonition or encouragement*

B
Bible Focus

> *You yourselves know, brethren, that our coming to you was not in vain. But even after we had suffered before and were spitefully treated at Philippi, as you know, we were bold in our God to speak to you the gospel of God in much conflict. For our exhortation did not come from error or uncleanness, nor was it in deceit. But as we have been approved by God to be entrusted with the gospel, even so we speak, not as pleasing men, but God who tests our hearts.*
>
> *For neither at any time did we use flattering words, as you know, nor a cloak for covetousness—God is witness. Nor did we seek glory from men, either from you or from others, when we might have made demands as apostles of Christ. But we were gentle among you, just as a nursing mother cherishes her own children.*
>
> *So, affectionately longing for you, we were well pleased to impart to you not only the gospel of God, but also our own lives, because you had became dear to us. For you remember, brethren, our labor and toil; for laboring night and day, that we might not be a burden to any of you, we preached to you the gospel of God.*
>
> *You are witnesses, and God also, how devoutly and justly and blamelessly we behaved ourselves among you who believe; as you know how we exhorted, and comforted, and charged every one of you, as a father does his own children, that you should walk worthy of God who calls you into His own kingdom and glory (1 Thess. 2:1–12).*

Paul boldly told the Thessalonians that there were certain things he and his preaching companions had *not* done in declaring the Gospel of Jesus Christ to them:

- They had not preached error or lie—rather, they had preached truth.

- They had not preached as men with impure lives or motives. Their lives validated their message and did not detract from it.

- They had not used flattering words in their preaching.

• They had not preached with the goal of financial extortion.

• They had not preached in order to be popular among the people.

Paul was also bold in declaring the virtuous way in which he and his fellow ministers, Silvanus (Silas) and Timothy, *had* behaved in their midst:

• They had been gentle and affectionate.

• They had labored night and day to earn their keep and not be a burden to anyone—they were not lazy in their efforts, nor did they display a sense of entitlement.

• They had exhibited devout, just, and blameless behavior.

• They had exhorted, comforted, and charged the Thessalonians—as "a father does his own children"—to walk worthy of God.

They came to the Thessalonians not to please them but to fulfill the call of God on their lives.

In these few short paragraphs, the apostle Paul gave a very clear profile of what it means to be a *true* minister of the Gospel. This profile applies not only to clergy, but to the laity. It applies to all who seek to minister to others the truth of the Gospel, or to disciple others in the faith. God calls all believers to spread the Gospel with a genuine love for others; a purity of message, motive, and behavior; and a simple proclamation of the truth.

Paul also made it clear in this passage that those who are persuaded to believe the Gospel that is preached to them have the privilege of evaluating the behavior of the preacher who bears the good news, including evaluating the preacher's message for any underlying motives. To those who say, "Don't look at my life, just listen to the truth of my words," Paul no doubt would have replied, "Look at my life—it adds validity to the truth of my words." From Paul's perspective, the Gospel must be presented in a way that is free of any overlay of deceit, manipulation of others, or attempt to sway others for financial gain.

Even as Paul called upon the Thessalonians to accurately evaluate their lives, he stated that he and his companions felt totally confident in this: "God is witness."

It would be easy to use this passage as a template for evaluating others. Rather, we are wise to use it as a template in evaluating ourselves.

Why do you pursue the ministry activities that you pursue? Why do you seek to influence others for Christ? What are your motives? Is your message totally without error, deceit, or manipulation? How do you know that it is? What do you feel toward those with whom you share your knowledge of

Christ Jesus? Are you willing for your life to be transparent to those you seek to influence for Christ?

The Thessalonians were exemplary and faithful believers who heard the gospel from exemplary and faithful preachers of God's truth, an important aspect of how believers grow into maturity and joy.

A
Application for Today

There's a popular phrase among motivational speakers that proclaims: "People don't care how much you know until they know how much you care."

We take for granted that this is a true statement, but *why* is it true? What are the implications in sharing the message of Christ Jesus?

There's another popular phrase that admonishes Christians to "walk the walk, and not just talk the talk."

We take this advice for granted, but why is this important? Is there a degree to which the truth of the gospel transcends the frailty of human nature and the flaws of human behavior? What are the unique challenges of walking and talking in integrity?

There's yet a third popular phrase that says, "Hate the sin but love the sinner."

We like the sound of this, but how do we do it? How can we love a person who is blatantly sinning, without seeming to accept their sin?

We hear repeatedly that it is wrong to tell others, "Do what I say, not as I do," especially when it comes to parenting.

Examine this closely. Why do children have the right to evaluate the behavior of their parents who give them instruction about what is right and wrong? Why do parishioners have the right to evaluate the behavior of their pastors who preach to them about truth and error? Do parishioners have the right to evaluate the behavior of a pastor's spouse or children?

How do you believe the apostle Paul would answer these four common phrases in our culture today?

• People don't care how much you know until they know how much you care.

• Walk the walk—don't just talk the talk.

• Hate the sin but love the sinner.

• Do what I say, not as I do.

S
Supplementary Scriptures to Consider

The apostle Paul placed high value on the fact that he and his ministry colleagues had paid their own way as they did the work of evangelists in Thessalonica:

> We command you, brethren, in the name of our Lord Jesus Christ, that you withdraw from every brother who walks disorderly and not according to the tradition which he received from us. For you yourselves know how you ought to follow us, for we were not disorderly among you; nor did we eat anyone's bread free of charge, but worked with labor and toil night and day, that we might not be a burden to any of you, not because we do not have authority, but to make ourselves an example of how you should follow us.
>
> For even when we were with you, we commanded you this: If anyone will not work, neither shall he eat. For we hear that there are some who walk among you in a disorderly manner, not working at all, but are busybodies. Now those who are such we command and exhort through our Lord Jesus Christ that they work in quietness and eat their own bread (2 Thess. 3:6–12).

• What does it mean to walk disorderly? What does it mean that some were not living "according to the tradition" they had received from Paul? What does it mean to us today? (Note: Read the rest of the cited passage for clues.)

- What does "work in quietness" mean?

- What does it mean, in very practical terms, to be a busybody?

- Name at least two reasons why it would be wise to refrain from association with disorderly people?

- What would be the implications for the broader society if this rule of Paul were applied universally: "If anyone will not work, neither shall he eat"?

Paul used two specific words to describe the way he wanted the Thessalonians to treat their leaders: *recognize* their leaders, and *esteem* them. To recognize meant to know, which is more than mere acknowledgement. To esteem is to value.

> We urge you, brethren, to recognize those who labor among
> you, and are over you in the Lord and admonish you, and to
> esteem them very highly in love for their work's sake. Be at
> peace among yourselves (1 Thess. 5:12–13).

• In what ways might a group of people come to recognize its leaders? What is the role of the leader in allowing himself or herself to be recognized? What is the role of the person seeking to know a leader?

• To what degree do you believe you know your pastor (or pastors)?

• In what ways does your church esteem its leaders? What are the appropriate ways of esteeming a leader? Inappropriate ways?

In both of the letters to the Thessalonians, Paul specifically requests prayer.

1. Brethren, pray for us (1 Thess. 5:25).

2. Brethren, pray for us, that the word of the Lord may run swiftly and be glorified, just as it is with you, and that we may be delivered from unreasonable and wicked men; for not all have faith (2 Thess. 3:1–2).

• Why is it important to ask those who follow you to pray for you?

• In what ways do Paul's requests for prayer reflect the profile of behavior and character that he identified in this chapter's opening Bible passage?

• How do our prayer requests reflect our heart's desires and character?

I
Introspection and Implications

1. How might you defend your ministry to other people? What profile of behavior and character would you claim for yourself?

2. In what ways do you feel challenged to adjust your attitude or behaviors as you pursue the ministry you believe God has called you to do?

3. To what degree are you willing to let others know you?

4. Is it a good idea for followers to become friends? Why or why not? What are some of the fears a person might need to face regarding allowing a follower to become a friend?

5. Does being transparent before others mean that a leader loses all privacy? Why or why not? What are the limitations or boundaries related to being transparent as a leader or minister?

C
Communicating the Good News

How important is it for a person who is sharing the Gospel of Jesus Christ to have integrity between motives and message? Why is simply telling a person your motives inadequate or unsatisfactory?

Why *do* you want another person to accept Jesus as Savior?

Why *do* you want another person to follow Jesus as Lord?

In what ways do you attempt to reveal your motives by your behavior?

LESSON #3

OVERCOMING SATAN'S HINDRANCES

Hinder: to obstruct or delay the progress or development of something or someone

B
Bible Focus

> But we, brethren, having been taken away from you for a
> short time in presence, not in heart, endeavored more eagerly
> to see your face with great desire. Therefore we wanted to
> come to you—even I, Paul, time and again—but Satan hin-
> dered us. For what is our hope, or joy, or crown of rejoicing?
> Is it not even you in the presence of our Lord Jesus Christ at
> His coming? For you are our glory and joy.
>
> Therefore, when we could no longer endure it, we thought it
> good to be left in Athens alone, and sent Timothy, our brother
> and minister of God, and our fellow laborer in the gospel of
> Christ, to establish you and encourage you concerning your
> faith, that no one should be shaken by these afflictions; for
> you yourselves know that we are appointed to this. For, in fact,
> we told you before when we were with you that we would
> suffer tribulation, just as it happened, and you know. For this
> reason, when I could no longer endure it, I sent to know your
> faith, lest by some means the tempter had tempted you, and
> our labor might be in vain.
>
> But now that Timothy has come to us from you, and brought
> us good news of your faith and love, and that you always have
> good remembrance of us, greatly desiring to see us, as we also
> to see you—therefore, brethren, in all our affliction and
> distress we were comforted concerning you by your faith. For
> now we live, if you stand fast in the Lord
> (1 Thess. 2:19–3:8).

Paul wanted to revisit the Thessalonians, and he earnestly desired that the
Thessalonians know that he wanted to revisit them. Even so, he did not
return to them. He was hindered in his efforts to travel to them, and he used
this hindrance to teach them and us about our limitations as Christians when
he comes to dealing with satan.

The simple truth is this: no matter how mature we might be in our faith,
we do not have definitive power over the enemy of our souls. Only Christ
Jesus has that power.

Our power is not the power of vanquishing conquest as much as it is the
power of resistance. The apostle James wrote: "Resist the devil and he will
flee from you" (James 4:7). The power of resistance lies in this: find a way
to keep moving forward.

The specific word hinder in the passage above refers to a military battle strategy, in which a group of people who are about to be invaded sabotages possible routes of travel in order to interrupt and delay an enemy army's advance. The understanding is that a battle will eventually occur, but the "hindering strategies" often work to delay the confrontation and weaken the morale of the approaching army.

The apostle Paul certainly wasn't about to be weakened in morale, but he was delayed. And whenever the enemy put up hindering resistance to Paul, he simply responded with greater intensity and drive. He resisted the resistance. He became stronger in purpose and even more motivated to accomplish his mission.

Paul understood that as Satan hindered him personally, he likely was seeking to stunt the spiritual growth of the Thessalonians. He saw the purpose of his travel delays as an attempt of the enemy to keep him from giving face-to-face encouragement and instruction. Paul wrote to say, "Don't let Satan discourage you, slow your growth, or damage your faith."

In the end, Paul found a way to get to the Thessalonians even if he could not get to Thessalonica: he wrote letters and sent Timothy. Was this Plan B just as effective—and perhaps even more so? Let history provide the answers. If Paul had gone to Thessalonica personally we might not have the recorded wisdom of the letters we know as 1 and 2 Thessalonians. In addition, Paul wrote that he was very encouraged by the good report Timothy brought back to him. That good report strengthened Paul to endure what he was experiencing in his personal life. Simultaneously, the Thessalonians had a renewed confidence that they were not reliant upon Paul and could trust God with their own faith to "stand fast in the Lord." Plan B was not a lesser plan, but a more effective plan.

We may be hindered.

But we must not allow ourselves to be *stopped* when it comes to fulfilling God's purposes for our lives.

We must meet the resistance of the enemy with an even greater resolve, relying upon the Lord to give us a creative and *better* plan for fulfilling our mission.

Are you being hindered today?

What course of action can you take to circumvent this hindrance?

A
Application for Today

"I think the devil's work is all about pressing," a woman shared with her friend over tea.

"Pressing?" her friend asked.

"He *press*es us with too many obligations and time commitments and responsibilities—and we call it *press*ure, or stress. And then he de*press*es us with too much sorrow and anxiety. He tries to im*press* us with temptations and evil thoughts. He op*press*es us with burdens that seem too heavy to carry. He com*press*es our vision for the world by getting us totally preoccupied with emergencies so that we get tunnel vision and focus only on the urgent and not the important. And all the while, he tries to sup*press* every effort to share the gospel with others. Press, press, press."

"So what do we do?" her friend sighed.

"Press back."

"But how?" her friend asked.

"I give Him a good dousing of Jesus."

"How on earth do you do that?"

"First, I tell the Lord in a loud voice exactly how much I want Him to destroy the devil—and I get pretty graphic in describing the ways I want Jesus to beat up on him. And then, I put on my loud praise voice, telling anyone and anything in earshot how great and glorious a Lord I serve. I give loud thanksgiving for what I believe Jesus is doing and is going to do. And, you know, I find that the devil gives up pretty quick.

"The old devil might have hindering power. But I have hallelujah power."

In what ways are you confronting the devil about the ways in which he may be confronting you?

In what ways are you resisting his hindrances?

S
Supplementary Scriptures to Consider

Paul had an ongoing desire to help perfect the faith of the steadfast Thessalonians. He did not allow satan's hindrance to weaken this desire or lessen his resolve.

> For what thanks can we render to God for you, for all the joy
> with which we rejoice for your sake before our God, night and
> day praying exceedingly that we may see your face and
> perfect what is lacking in your faith?
>
> Now may our God and Father Himself, and our Lord Jesus
> Christ, direct our way to you. And may the Lord make you
> increase and abound in love to one another and to all, just as
> we do to you, so that He may establish your hearts blameless
> in holiness before our God and Father at the coming of our
> Lord Jesus Christ with all His saints (1 Thess. 3:9–13).

- What do you perceive may still be "lacking in your faith"? Is there an area where you struggle to trust God completely? Is there an area of question or doubt in which you struggle to know the truth? How might you address these areas of lack in your faith?

- What does it mean to "increase and abound in love to one another and to all"? Is there a way in which we love others in the church differently than we love others in the world?

- How do you believe the Lord desires to establish your heart "blameless in holiness"?

• What is the connection between abounding in love for one another and being established blameless in holiness?

Paul was very clear that it is the *Lord's* work to establish us, guard us, and direct us:

> The Lord is faithful, who will establish you and guard you from the evil one. And we have confidence in the Lord concerning you, both that you do and will do the things we command you.
> Now may the Lord direct your hearts into the love of God and into the patience of Christ (2 Thess. 3:3–5).

• What does it mean to be established spiritually? What does it mean to have full assurance that the Lord is faithful in establishing you?

• What does it mean to be "guarded from the evil one"? What are the limitations the Lord places on the way the devil deals with you?

• What does it mean to have your heart "directed" toward the love of God and the patience of Christ?

• Paul wrote that the "Lord is faithful" in establishing, guarding, and directing us. What does it mean to rely totally upon the Lord to establish, guard, and direct us—rather than seek to establish, guard, and direct ourselves? How difficult is it to rely fully on the faithfulness of the Lord in these areas?

I
Introspection and Implications

1. When hindered in their ministry efforts, many people simply give up rather than seek an even more potent Plan B. How do you deal with hindrances? How do you avoid the temptation to give up?

2. How do you discern whether a hindrance is Satan's work, or God leading you to a different plan? If a person remains intent on seeking God's *best* plan in any given circumstance—a plan that is effective in producing godly results—is it even important to discern the reason for Plan A's failure? Why or why not?

3. How do you draw strength and encouragement by hearing good news about the ways other believers prosper, endure, or grow in their faith? Why is it important that you share what God is doing in your life with those who led you to the Lord or with those who have mentored or influenced you to grow spiritually?

C
Communicating the Good News

Is there a worn-out evangelism tactic that no longer seems to be working for you or your church? How might you come together to discern a new approach to evangelism?

In what ways might you and others in your church unite in your efforts to resist the current hindering factors that satan seems to have instigated against you?

LESSON #4

ABOUNDING MORE
AND MORE

*Abound: to have something in
large amount, quantity, or number*

B
Bible Focus

> We urge and exhort in the Lord Jesus that you should
> abound more and more, just as you received from us how you
> ought to walk and to please God; for you know what com-
> mandments we gave you through the Lord Jesus.
>
> For this is the will of God, your sanctification: that you
> should abstain from sexual immorality; that each of you
> should know how to possess his own vessel in sanctification
> and honor, not in passion of lust, like the Gentiles who do not
> know God; that no one should take advantage of and defraud
> his brother in this matter, because the Lord is the avenger of
> all such, as we also forewarned you and testified. For God did
> not call us to uncleanness, but in holiness. Therefore he who
> rejects this does not reject man, but God, who has also given
> us His Holy Spirit.
>
> But concerning brotherly love you have no need that I
> should write to you, for you yourselves are taught by God to
> love one another; and indeed you do so toward all the breth-
> ren who are in all Macedonia. But we urge you, brethren, that
> you increase more and more; that you also aspire to lead a
> quiet life, to mind your own business, and to work with your
> own hands, as we commanded you, that you may walk prop-
> erly toward those who are outside, and that you may lack
> nothing (1 Thess. 4:1–12).

More and more, and increasingly more. That is what the apostle Paul
desired for the Thessalonians. Note quickly, however, that this acquisition of
more was not outward or material in nature. Rather, it was an inner spiritual
work focused on moral character.

Throughout Paul's letters we find a subtle theme: those who are increasingly filled and influenced by the Holy Spirit have *less* capacity for being
filled with the lusts of human nature and the influences of the world, led by
the Spirit to spiritually right actions have less propensity to sin. As human
beings, we are vessels with a capacity for moral character. We will be filled
either by our own lusts and desires and live as "natural man," or we will
submit ourselves to being filled by God's Spirit and live as "spiritual man."

Consider the metaphor of a large container that has been filled with a
poisonous liquid. If that container is placed over a drain suitable for handling

toxic substances, and then fresh pure water is allowed to run into and over-flow the container, over time and depending on the force of the inflowing water, the poison will be eliminated from the container. Initially, the poison is simply diluted, but as the water continues to run with sufficient cleansing force, it replaces the poison. Eventually, only pure water fills the container. Such is the work of the Holy Spirit flooding into our lives and cleansing us from all sin and unrighteous impulses. The theological word for the process is *sanctification,* which means to be purified and made suitable for holy purposes.

The Thessalonian believers had been steeped in the poison of Greek immorality and promiscuity. Paul encouraged them to allow the Spirit to transform them and to purify them of the lusts and passions that would lead them to sin against one another.

In addition, the Thessalonians were steeped in a culture that was ex-tremely competitive and manipulative. Those who lived along the major trade routes were highly focused on buying at the lowest possible price and selling at the highest possible price. The Thessalonians loved to laud win-ners, and most Greeks aspired to do as little as possible for the maximum amount of praise and recognition. They held to a perspective, "If you can get another person to run your con and produce a profit for you, let that person serve your purposes." Paul encouraged the believers to allow the Spirit to impart to them a new lifestyle marked by quiet steadfastness, honorable transactions, and personal responsibility.

In matters of sexual morality and godly living, the Thessalonians were challenged to develop a purity of brotherly love for one another. And what benefits were they taught to expect? Good relationships with those outside the church and a sufficiency of supply for all their personal material needs.

In simple terms, Paul presented these principles to the Thessalonians:

• More of God. Less of self.

• More of God's love and supply. Less strife and need.

These are principle to be learned by every Christian in every age and culture.

What do you believe God desires to produce more of in your life? Are you willing to let Him do so?

How, in practical real-life ways, are you submitting yourself to His sanctifying processes?

A
Application for Today

"What are your aspirations?" a grandfather asked his grandson who had recently graduated from college.

The grandson quickly rattled off a list of goals that included securing a high-profile, high-paying job; getting married and having children; owning a home; and starting a financial portfolio for retirement. He included goals of becoming a leader in the church, getting involved in community activities, and perhaps even running for political office one day.

"In other words," the grandfather said, "you want to be rich, famous, powerful, a family man . . . and godly, too?"

The grandson laughed. "Sure. I want it all."

"You've described a life that will take a lot of work," the grandfather said. "Are you aware that the word *aspire* means to be industrious, to work hard and stay focused?"

"I'm willing to work hard."

"Can I give you a little grandfatherly wisdom?" the grandfather asked.

"Sure, Grandpa," the young man said. "I value the advice you give me. I always have."

The grandfather smiled and nodded. "Then remember this, my boy. The real question is not how hard you are willing to work, but whether you are willing to let God work in you. Even as you make a living, you must be willing to let Him make your life."

What are your aspirations?

Are they in line with God's call to purity and righteousness?

Are they aspirations that produce genuine brotherly love? A quiet life? A life that is pleasing to God?

S
Supplementary Scriptures to Consider

Paul also wrote of abounding in love in his second letter to the Thessalonians:

> We . . . thank God always for you, brethren, as it is fitting, because your faith grows exceedingly, and the love of every one of you all abounds toward each other, so that we ourselves boast of you among the churches of God for your patience and faith in all your persecutions and tribulations that you endure (2 Thess. 1:3–4).

• Describe a situation in which you believe love "abounded" from one believer to another or from one group of believers to other people?

• Paul described the abounding love of the Thessalonians as manifesting itself in the midst of persecutions and tribulations. What impact does a hard time have on personal relationships? Is love more likely to be shown or less likely? Why?

• Paul commended the Thessalonians for their patience and faith. How are these character qualities linked to love?

Peter wrote specifically about perfecting moral character and the blessing this produces:

> Giving all diligence, add to your faith virtue, to virtue knowl-
> edge, to knowledge self-control, to self-control perseverance,
> to perseverance godliness, to godliness brotherly kindness, and
> to brotherly kindness love. For if these things are yours and
> abound, you will be neither barren nor unfruitful in the
> knowledge of our Lord Jesus Christ (2 Pet. 1:5–8).

• The link is made between the increase of spiritual character and a growing "knowledge" of Christ. In what ways have you come to "know
  Christ" better the more you have allowed the Holy Spirit to produce His
  character likeness in you?

• The link is also made in these verses between the increase of spiritual
  character and effectiveness of ministry. In what ways do you recognize
  that your ministry efforts have become more powerful and effective the
  more you have allowed the Spirit to purify your moral character?

The book of Proverbs gives this nugget of wisdom:

> A faithful man will abound with blessings, but he who hastens
> to be rich will not go unpunished (Prov. 28:20).

- What do you believe to be the blessings for those who are faithful?

- To be rich means to have more, to have great quantity or abundance. Those who "hasten to be rich" are those who are self-motivated to the point that they will do whatever it takes to produce gain, even to the point of unrighteous behavior. In what ways are their aspirations thwarted by God? Can you cite an example of this?

- What is the difference between trusting God to produce blessings in us and make our lives a blessing to others, and attempting to acquire blessings or be a blessing solely by our own efforts?

I
Introspection and Implications

1. What does it mean to "aspire to lead a quiet life"? How difficult is it to do this in a society that seems more bent on contention than on being content? What do you believe are the hallmarks of a quiet, peaceful, contented life?

2. What does it mean to "mind your own business"? What are the challenges in refraining from meddling in the business of others? What is the balance between caring for others and requiring them to take responsibility for their own lives?

3. What does it mean to "work with your own hands"?

4. What are the foremost challenges you face in submitting yourself to receiving more and more of the Spirit of God?

5. Do you consider yourself to be sanctified? Why or why not?

C
Communicating the Good News

How does sexual purity enhance a person's witness of Jesus as Savior and Lord?

In what ways does a godly approach to business and work enhance a person's witness of Jesus as Savior and Lord?

Sexual impropriety and financial malfeasance are among the foremost denunciations against the church today. Why do you believe these two types of sin seem to be such strong enemies of the Gospel?

What more might be done to ensure that your church remains free of sexual sin and greed?

LESSON #5
READY FOR CHRIST'S COMING

*Comfort: bring relief from
distress or anxiety*

B
Bible Focus

I do not want you to be ignorant, brethren, concerning those who have fallen asleep, lest you sorrow as others who have no hope. For if we believe that Jesus died and rose again, even so God will bring with Him those who sleep in Jesus.

For this we say to you by the word of the Lord, that we who are alive and remain until the coming of the Lord will by no means precede those who are asleep. For the Lord Himself will descend from heaven with a shout, with the voice of an archangel, and with the trumpet of God. And the dead in Christ will rise first. Then we who are alive and remain shall be caught up together with them in the clouds to meet the Lord in the air. And thus we shall always be with the Lord. Therefore comfort one another with these words.

But concerning the time and the seasons, brethren, you have no need that I should write to you. For you yourselves know perfectly that the day of the Lord so comes as a thief in the night. For when they say, "Peace and safety," then sudden destruction comes upon them, as labor pains upon a pregnant woman. And they shall not escape. But you, brethren, are not in darkness, so that this Day should overtake you as a thief. You are all sons of light and sons of the day. We are not of the night nor of darkness. Therefore let us not sleep, as others do, but let us watch and be sober. For those who sleep, sleep at night, and those who get drunk are drunk at night. But let us who are of the day be sober, putting on the breastplate of faith and love, and as a helmet the hope of salvation. For God did not appoint us to wrath, but to obtain salvation through our Lord Jesus Christ, who died for us, that whether we wake or sleep, we should live together with Him.

Therefore comfort each other and edify one another, just as you also are doing (1 Thess. 4:13–5:11).

The first-century church eagerly anticipated the return of Jesus in what came to be called the second coming. The new believers in Thessalonica— as was true of believers across the region—desired to know Jesus in *fullness*. They craved knowing Him as the apostles knew Him. They longed for Him to establish His kingdom and usher in a reign of righteousness to replace the systems of their sin-sick world. True believers today are no less eager for Christ's return.

The apostle Paul reinforced three messages to the Thessalonians:

First, those who have already died in Christ and those who are alive when Christ returns will be reunited, and together, they will "always be with the Lord." Questions apparently had arisen in Thessalonica about whether one group might have priority or precedence over the other. No, Paul explained, we will be gathered together in the Lord.

Second, we cannot know precisely when Christ will return but we can know this: He will come quickly and unexpectedly. And He will not come according to the predictions of man, but according to the timing established by God the Father. Just as a baby in the womb eventually comes to the hour of birthing, so the Day of the Lord will come as an inevitable, God-authorized event in human history.

Third, no one will escape the judgment that occurs as part of Christ's return. Those who have chosen to live in the darkness of sin and separation from God's love will live perpetually in darkness and separation. Those who have chosen to live in the light of Christ will continue to live in the light of His presence for all eternity. Believers do not need to fear the Day of the Lord. Those who are fully living in the Lord will simply continue to live in Him, only with greater fullness and joy . . . forever.

Paul made it clear that these words of instruction were intended to give the Thessalonians hope and comfort. The Greeks tended to think of hope as a wishful projection about an uncertain future. The New Testament under-standing of hope, however, is different. Hope is rooted in a confident assurance that God will keep every one of His promises. The future is based upon past action, and for the Christian the actions of Jesus Christ dying on a cross and rising from the dead are what *ensure* that what God has promised *will happen*. Hope, therefore, is not wishful thinking, but an expectation for the fulfillment of a certain future. Knowing that our future in Christ is assured gives comfort. Christians are not to live with unfounded optimism but in eager anticipation of an established reality about to be revealed.

Finally, Paul admonished the Thessalonians to watch and to be sober. They were to be on the alert, ever ready for Christ's return. They were to live with serious intention, preparing themselves for a glorious union with Christ and reunion with their departed loved ones.

What good words these are for us today as we, too, anticipate the second coming of Christ. We do not need to fear Christ's return. Neither should we ever think that He may not return. Our comfort lies in knowing that Christ will come again, and when He does, we will be reunited with all other believers through the ages for an eternity in God's near presence.

What emotions does the phrase "Second Coming of Christ" evoke in you?

Do you believe you are fully ready for His return?
If you do not feel ready, what might you do to become ready?

A
Application for Today

"Is it Christmas today?"

The little girl had asked her parents this same question for ten straight days. Alas, the calendar said "December 18." There was still an entire week before Christmas.

"No," Mom and Dad said. "You need to be patient. Christmas will come soon."

They knew their little girl was too young to understand calendars or the length of a week. She couldn't count yet, so even trying to calculate Christmas in terms of number of "sleeps" wouldn't work.

At the mention of the word *patient*, the little girl sighed and then walked away to play cheerfully with a bucket of brightly colored ribbons and bows her mother had given her to decorate her toys.

One night her parents began to reflect on their daughter's eagerness for Christmas. "I want to have the same excitement about the return of Christ that our little girl has about the coming of Christmas," said Mom.

"I agree," said Dad. "But there's something we probably need to learn from our daughter on this."

"What's that?" asked Mom.

"Our little girl isn't into date-setting," Dad said. "The fact that it *isn't* Christmas today has no impact on her delight in the Christmas tree lights or her wide-eyed eagerness to hear the Christmas story read to her one more time before she goes to bed. It doesn't matter to her that Christmas hasn't come today. She lives with undiminished hope that it just might come tomorrow."

"I think I see your point," Mom said. "On the one hand, many people today seem overly concerned about timetables and conjectures related to end-times events. On the other hand, some people don't seem to believe Christ is coming back—at least not in a real, physical sense. Neither group seems to have much joy."

"And that's the point." said Dad. "One of these days when our daughter asks, 'Is it Christmas today?' we will say, 'Yes.' And one of these days, it will be the day Christ returns. And until then, every day should be a day of living in the joyful anticipation and hope that Christ *is* coming for us."

Do you truly believe Christ is coming again?

Do you believe He might come tomorrow? Why or why not?

Would you live today differently if you knew with certainty that Jesus was returning tomorrow?

S
Supplementary Scriptures to Consider

Jesus had a number of things to say about His coming again. This passage relates to His appearance:

> [Jesus said,] "Then the sign of the Son of Man will appear in heaven, and then all the tribes of the earth will mourn, and they will see the Son of Man coming on the clouds of heaven with power and great glory.
>
> "And He will send His angels with a great sound of a trumpet, and they will gather together His elect from the four winds, from one end of heaven to the other" (Matt. 24:30–31).

• What images come to your mind when you think about Jesus coming "with power and great glory"?

• Why do you believe the "tribes of the earth will mourn" at Christ's return? How might this relate to the apostle Paul's words to the Thessalonians that "sudden destruction" will come upon those who are in darkness?

Jesus taught this about anticipating His return:

> [Jesus said,] "Now learn this parable from the fig tree: When its branch has already become tender and puts forth leaves, you know that summer is near.
>
> "So you also, when you see all these things, know that it is near—at the doors.
>
> "Assuredly, I say to you, this generation will by no means pass away till all these things take place.
>
> "Heaven and earth will pass away, but My words will by no means pass away" (Matt. 24:32–35).

• In what ways does living with a sense of immediacy about the Lord's return refine our behavior and keep us focused on those things that are truly of eternal importance?

• Jesus pointed to the importance of trusting in what will *not* pass away, rather than focusing on what *will* pass away. What does the phrase, "My words will by no means pass away" mean to you? Compare the certainty of God's Word with the speculations of men.

Jesus taught this about the timing of His return:

> [Jesus said,] "But of that day and hour no one knows, not even the angels of heaven, but My Father only.
>
> "Buy as the days of Noah were, so also will the coming of the Son of Man be.
>
> "For as in the days before the flood, they were eating and drinking, marrying and giving in marriage, until the day that Noah entered the ark,
>
> "and did not know until the flood came and took them all away, so also will the coming of the Son of Man be. . . .
>
> "Watch therefore, for you do not know what hour your Lord is coming" (Matt. 24:36–39, 42).

• From the account in Genesis, it appears that it took Noah a hundred years to build the ark. He and his family were sealed up in the ark for seven days before the rains began. How difficult would it be to continue to live in anticipation of a great flood during decades of no rain? How difficult would it be to live in a sealed-up ark for a full week without so much as a raindrop?

• What is the balance between living a normal daily life of routines and responsibilities and living on the keen edge of anticipation that all things may end tomorrow?

- How does this passage from Matthew relate to the apostle Paul's admonition to watch and be sober about the Lord's return?

I
Introspection and Implications

1. If you knew that the Lord's return was *imminent*, would you live any differently? Why or why not? If you would live differently, what keeps you from living or acting in that way *now*?

2. Are you driven by deadlines? To what extent is this a good thing? A bad thing?

3. What do you still hope to accomplish before the second coming of Christ?

4. Do Paul's words about the Day of the Lord give you comfort and hope? Why or why not?

C
Communicating the Good News

Do you believe the world as a whole is immune to the message, "The end of the world is near"?

What role do you believe the topic of the second coming of Christ should have in evangelism messages?

Lesson #6

RESISTANCE TO APOSTASY

Apostasy: renunciation of faith in Christ Jesus

B
Bible Focus

> Now, brethren, concerning the coming of our Lord Jesus
> Christ and our gathering together to Him, we ask you, not to
> be soon shaken in mind or troubled, either by spirit or by
> word or by letter, as if from us, as though the day of Christ
> had come. Let no one deceive you by any means; for that Day
> will not come unless the falling away comes first, and the man
> of sin is revealed, the son of perdition, who opposes and exalts
> himself above all that is called God or that is worshiped, so
> that he sits as God in the temple of God, showing himself that
> he is God.
>
> Do you not remember that when I was still with you I told
> you these things? And now you know what is restraining, that
> he may be revealed in his own time. For the mystery of law-
> lessness is already at work; only He who now restrains will do
> so until He is taken out of the way. And then the lawless one
> will be revealed, whom the Lord will consume with the breath
> of His mouth and destroy with the brightness of His coming.
> The coming of the lawless one is according to the working of
> Satan, with all power, signs, and lying wonders, and with all
> unrighteous deception among those who perish, because they
> did not receive the love of the truth, that they might be saved.
> And for this reason God will send them strong delusion, that
> they should believe the lie, that they all may be condemned
> who did not believe the truth but had pleasure in unrighteous-
> ness.
>
> But we are bound to give thanks to God always for you,
> brethren, beloved by the Lord, because God from the begin-
> ning chose you for salvation through sanctification by the
> Spirit and believe in the truth, to which He called you by our
> gospel, for the obtaining of the glory of our Lord Jesus Christ.
> Therefore, brethren, stand fast and hold the traditions which
> you were taught, whether by word or our epistle.
>
> Now may our Lord Jesus Christ Himself, and our God and
> Father, who has loved us and given us everlasting consolation
> and good by hope by grace, comfort your hearts and establish
> you in every good word and work (2 Thess. 2:1–17).

The apostle Paul wrote to the Thessalonians a second time to clarify his
teachings about the second coming of Christ. False teachers had apparently
come into the church proclaiming that the Day of the Lord had already

come. No, Paul wrote. And then he went on to describe two main things that would happen before that Day occurred.

First, there would be a great "falling away." The Greek word for this is *apostasia*, the word from which apostasy comes. This "falling away" is not a passive event, nor is it a simple matter of attrition or a decline in church attendance. Apostasy is an active, fervent, open rebellion against God. On a widespread basis, people not only will reject God and refuse to have anything to do with the worship of God, but they will oppose God and fight against all who *do* worship the Lord. They will set up human systems to worship and obey in place of God's commandments.

Second, there will be the rising up of a "man of sin." He is neither satan nor a superhuman being, but a man who will have a tremendous power to require others to engage in "lawlessness," which is the opposite of God's law. This man is described elsewhere in the New Testament as "the beast" (Rev. 13:1–10) and the Antichrist (1 John 2:18). He will embody all active and wicked resistance to Christ Jesus, and his human systems will produce signs and "lying wonders" as he draws power from satan. The apostle Paul is quick to assure the Thessalonians that he will be destroyed at the return of Christ (2 Thess. 2:8).

What troubles many about Paul's message is his reference to the "mystery of lawlessness," which includes an implication that God is the author of a "strong delusion" that causes many people to believe the lies of man and be condemned. People ask, "How can a loving God create forces that lead people to damnation?"

The key to the answer lies in a more complete understanding of God's universal and unchanging laws that have been in effect since Creation.

God is the author of all laws that govern our universe, whether natural, psychological, or spiritual. One of God's laws, for example, is the law of gravity. A person who walks off the edge of a cliff will fall, and unless he is able to grab hold of something on the way down, he will continue to fall until he can fall no further. A falling person will find it increasingly difficult to stop his fall the further he falls, and as a corollary principle, increasingly difficult to climb back up the face of the cliff. The forces of gravity will continue to pull the falling person toward the bottom of the ravine, and the greater the distance of the fall, the greater the harm to the person.

In similar manner, one of God's unchanging laws is called "the mystery of lawlessness." In accordance with this law, if a person chooses to believe and follow a specific line of lie—in this case, a lie about the necessity for sold-out obedience to God—that person will find it very easy to believe and embrace a second lie related to the first, and then a third lie, a fourth lie, and so forth. A fall from obedience and righteousness will have begun. As a person begins to act on the basis of lie, the person simultaneously will find it more and more difficult to perceive and believe the truth.

The more a person follows lies that result in rebellion against God, the more the person will become entrenched in rebellion, to the point that he will be totally incapable of discerning the truth. The end result will be complete delusion, leading to open warfare against God. The end consequence of that behavior is destruction. This is a *mystery* in that we do not fully understand *why* God would establish such a law or *why* a person would choose man-made ideas over God's ideas. Nevertheless, we see evidence all around us of this law in effect. You no doubt can cite many examples of people, even some church leaders, who are in a downward spiral of lawlessness in our world today.

God does not *desire* man to fall into a destructive pattern of believing lies that produce open rebellion, any more than God desires for a man to walk off a cliff. Human beings, however, have the free will to choose. God's laws apply universally, and the consequence associated with believing a string of rebellious lies is irreversible.

An awareness of this universal law gives us all the more reason to heed Paul's admonition that we "believe in the truth" and "stand fast and hold the traditions" of truth that we have been taught. Holding fast to the truth is what keeps us walking as far away from the edge of a spiritual cliff as possible. As we pursue the truth, we can be assured and comforted that God will *establish us* in every good word and work. We also can take comfort that we will not fall prey to the man of sin or become apostate.

What signs today do you see of people falling away from God's law and believing the lies of lawlessness that produce rebellion against God, His Word, and His people?

A
Application for Today

The little boy fell asleep in the car as the family drove home after the evening church service. The winter night was especially dark, and it was late. The boy's father carried him into the house and turned on the bright light in the little boy's bathroom to help him undress for bed. The boy started to open his eyes and then shut them tightly. "It's too bright! It's too bright!" he exclaimed, putting up his hands to cover his closed eyes.

The father responded quickly, understanding the problem. He turned off the overhead light and switched on a small lamp a few feet away in the adjacent bedroom. "Try now," he said to his son. The boy opened his eyes cautiously. "I'm not blind now," he said with great relief. "I can see ok, Daddy."

A person who is in darkness for a prolonged time adjusts to seeing in the dark. In similar manner, those who live in sin often adjust to living in sin and find it more comfortable and easier to live in sin rather than deal with the challenges related to living in righteousness. This seems to be especially so if a person has surrounded himself with other people who prefer sinful life patterns over godly ones.

Do you know anyone who has been living in the darkness of sin for so long that he or she seems to prefer sin and its consequences than to pursue or experience a life without sin? In what ways is such a person seemingly set up to continue to pursue sin? In what ways does such a person seem almost incapable of knowing or responding to the truth?

A tendency may exist for a person to conclude that God has caused the person to sin, or that God has relegated the person to a condemned life. Is this the work of God? Or is it the inevitable result of a long pattern of willful pursuit of sin?

S
Supplementary Scriptures to Consider

The book of James gives us full assurance that God does not entice people to sin, nor does He deceive:

> Let no one say when he is tempted, "I am tempted by God";
> for God cannot be tempted by evil, nor does He Himself tempt
> anyone. But each one is tempted when he is drawn away by
> his own desires and enticed. Then, when desire has conceived,
> it gives birth to sin; and sin, when it is full-grown, brings forth
> death (James 1:13–15).

• In what ways have you been enticed by your own desires to do things that are contrary to God's law? In times when you have given in to a specific temptation, have you found that it is easier to yield to that temptation a second time, a third time, and perhaps eventually to adopt a pattern of yielding repeatedly to that particular temptation? What was the result? How did you break that pattern of temptation? If you have not yet broken that pattern of temptation, what do you believe will be required for you to do so?

• Why is it important to recognize that God does not tempt us? (Note: Can you trust a person to deliver you if you also believe that person is eager to destroy you?)

The beast described in Revelation embodies a number of powers and abilities that are already evident in godless people today, only to a lesser degree.

> He opened his mouth in blasphemy against God, to blaspheme
> His name, His tabernacle, and those who dwell in heaven. It
> was granted to him to make war with the saints and to over-
> come them. And authority was given him over every tribe,
> tongue, and nation. All who dwell on the earth will worship
> him, whose names have not been written in the book of Life
> of the Lamb slain from the foundation of the world
> (Rev. 13:6–8).

- To blaspheme is to voice utter disrespect for God and the things of God. In what ways have you encountered blasphemy of God in your world?

- To blaspheme God's tabernacle is tantamount to blaspheming God's church. Have you encountered blasphemy of the church?

- To blaspheme "those who dwell in heaven" is to insult and voice utter disrespect for the lives and influences of deceased godly people. In what ways have you encountered blasphemy of those who accomplished great things for God during their lifetimes?

The apostle Paul was quick to encourage the Thessalonians that their godly lives would be rewarded and that God would one day judge and destroy their enemies:

> We are bound to thank God always for you, brethren, as it is fitting, because your faith grows exceedingly, and the love of every one of you all abounds toward each other, so that we ourselves boast of you among the churches of God for your patience and faith in all your persecutions and tribulations that you endure, which is manifest evidence of the righteous judgment of God, that you may be counted worthy of the kingdom of God, for which you also suffer; since it is a righteous thing with God to repay with tribulation those who trouble you, and to give you who are troubled rest with us when the Lord Jesus is revealed from heaven with His mighty angels, in flaming fire taking vengeance on those who do not know God, and on those who do not obey the gospel of our Lord Jesus Christ. These shall be punished with everlasting destruction from the presence of the Lord and from the glory of His power, when He comes, in that Day, to be glorified in His saints and to be admired among all those who believe, because our testimony among you was believed
> (2 Thess. 1:3–11).

• Paul noted that the Thessalonians' growing and enduring faith and their love for one another made them worthy of the kingdom of God. Would Paul write these same words of encouragement to your church? Why or why not?

• In what ways can a person develop growing and enduring faith? Is exercising faith in the face of persecution part of the way faith grows?

• What fate does the apostle Paul declare for those who do not know God or who are disobedient to the gospel of the Lord Jesus Christ? Does this give you comfort or create anxiety in you? Why?

I
Introspection and Implications

1. Do you see examples of apostasy in our world today? Focus on one example and describe it. How do you believe this apostasy might be confronted?

2. How do we as believers keep from falling into lies that lead to apostasy? How do we protect our children, new believers, and the spiritually innocent among us from the lies that cause a person to choose lawlessness over God's law?

3. Those who teach government agents about counterfeit money do not focus on counterfeit bills in their instruction. Rather, they present only *genuine* bills for detailed examination, and they teach the agents all of the undeniable earmarks of a real piece of currency. How does this principle relate to the apostle Paul's challenge to "stand fast and hold the traditions which you were taught, whether by word or our epistle" (2 Thess. 2:15)?

C
Communicating the Good News

How can the church best reach out to those who are falling away into lies that produce rebellion against God?

LESSON #7

ADMONITIONS
AND BLESSINGS

*Admonish: to rebuke or advise someone mildly
but earnestly to do something or
not do something*

B
Bible Focus

> *Now we exhort you, brethren, warn those who are unruly,*
> *comfort the fainthearted, uphold the weak, be patient with all.*
> *See that no one renders evil for evil to anyone, but always*
> *pursue what is good both for yourselves and for all.*
> *Rejoice always, pray without ceasing, in everything give*
> *thanks; for this is the will of God in Christ Jesus for you.*
> *Do not quench the Spirit. Do not despise prophecies. Test*
> *all things; hold fast what is good. Abstain from every form of*
> *evil.*
> *Now may the God of peace Himself sanctify you com-*
> *pletely; and may your whole spirit, soul, and body be*
> *preserved blameless at the coming of our Lord Jesus Christ.*
> *He who calls you is faithful, who also will do it (1 Thess.*
> *5:14–24).*

In just a few short statements, the apostle Paul answered three great questions that have faced most bodies of believers throughout the ages.

Question #1: How do we to treat "problem people" in the church? Paul identified three types of people that can be found in virtually every congregation of significant size. Keep in mind that people with these problems can and likely will create problems for others:

- *The unruly.* When it comes to those who are troublemakers or who always seek to challenge the rules of the church or commands of God, Paul said, "Warn them." Don't ignore or dismiss their behavior. Confront their error. Warnings are always linked to consequences. Be direct in telling the unruly what their continued unruly behavior will produce.

- *The fainthearted.* When it comes to those who are on the verge of giving up and walking away because the Christian life seems too difficult, Paul said, "Comfort them." Surround them with warm godly friendship and prayer and stand with them. Help them to make the difficult choices related to living for Christ Jesus.

- *The weak.* When it comes to those who are either too young or too spiritually immature to stand strong in their faith, Paul said, "Uphold them." Teach them and train them in the ways of God so that they will know fully what they believe and why.

In dealing with all people in the church Paul said, "Pursue what is for the common good." In pursuing what is good for all who are in the church, you will inevitably pursue what is good for yourself. The converse is to be avoided: those who pursue what is only good for themselves usually miss what is good for the entire body.

In all relationships, we are to be patient with others, even as God is patient with us.

Question #2: How can we know the will of God? While each person may have a specific role to fill, the *general* will of God is the same for all believers: give praise to God (which is what it means to rejoice), ask God continually for everything you need, and give thanks to God regardless of your outer circumstances. We thank God for what He has done, is doing, and promises to do. Our expressions of thanks are as personal as our unique lives and as current as today. We praise God for Who He is—which never changes. We ask God for provision, protection, and peace, which may be stated in terms of wholeness. We do this according to the challenges and needs we are facing at any given time. God promises to respond to our thanks, praise, and prayers in ways that will always be for our eternal benefit.

If someone asks, "What is God's will for my life?" you can always respond with confidence, "God's will for you is that you rejoice always, pray always, and give thanks in every situation."

Question #3: How can we stay on God's path and avoid falling into error? Paul gave four overriding principles:

- *Don't quench the Spirit.* Rather, ask the Holy Spirit to lead and guide you daily and in all decisions. Don't trust your own wisdom. Instead, turn to the all-wise Spirit of Truth as your counselor.

- *Don't despise prophecies.* The prophetic word of God is not a prediction about the future nearly as much as it is a proclamation about the truth of God that transcends all circumstances, situations, and times. Hear the preached Word of God. Learn and apply God's principles so they produce the trends of your overall life and lead to your blessing and fulfillment of purpose.

- *Test all things.* Put everything you hear and read to the test of God's Word. Does a statement line up with Scripture? If not, discard it. Do a person's motives line up with Christ's character? If not, beware. We have been given the ability to discern good from evil, but we must be intentional about discernment. When we know what is good, we must cling to it and refuse to allow it to become compromised. We must quickly discard what we know to be a lie or a temptation to sin.

- *Abstain from every form of evil.* Don't dabble with what God's Word declares is evil. Say no to every temptation to try out sin.

The good news is that we *can* live godly lives, fulfill the will of God, and be part of strong faithful churches. In the end, the perfecting of our lives is God's work. We do what He tells us to do, and He does what He says He will do: purify us until we are blameless.

Individually or collectively as a church, have you asked the three questions above? How does Paul's wisdom apply to your unique situation?

A
Application for Today

"I don't want any pie-in-the-sky stuff," the man said gruffly to his pastor. "You know I'm a practical man and I want the bottom line. Don't tell me to be good or live godly. Give me a list of practical ways to be good. Tell me what works to make me godly."

The pastor knew that the man speaking to him had accepted Jesus as his Savior. The pastor also had the benefit of having known the man and his family since they had been boys together in elementary school.

The pastor said, "Alright. Give me a day or two on this. I'm going to write out a prescription for you." This is what the pastor eventually wrote:

Rx for Sam

Every morning do these five things:
1. Say out loud ten things you are thankful for.

2. Praise God for one of His attributes (example: healer, savior, helper).

3. Ask God for what you believe the most important thing you need in the day ahead.

4. Ask the Holy Spirit to help you make right decisions and choices.

5. Read the Bible for ten minutes and ask God to show you how to apply what you read to your life.

During the day do these things:
1. Find one practical way to be a friend to your wife Mary and find one way to be a mentor to your children or your business associates. Help out or teach what you know every chance you get.

2. If anybody lies to you, respond by speaking the truth. If the person tries to get you to sin, refuse.

3. If somebody says or does something good to you, thank the person and receive what they say or give.

Finally: read this list every day and do it.

Sam did what his pastor and friend said to do. His children found "Rx to Sam" in his wallet after Sam died. The prescription was yellowed and well-worn. "That was the way Dad lived." one of the children exclaimed.

And the Rx for Sam became the eulogy for Sam's funeral.

What Rx are you following for your life?

S
Supplementary Scriptures to Consider

The apostle Paul knew that one of the greatest challenges faced by any believer is the challenge to love those who act in unlovable ways.

> As for you brethren, do not grow weary in doing good. And if anyone does not obey our word in this epistle, note that person and do not keep company with him, that he may be ashamed. Yet do not count him as an enemy, but admonish him as a brother (2 Thess. 3:13–15).

• Why are we wise never to dismiss the actions of those who are disobedient to God's Word?

• How do you "admonish" a person "as a brother"?

- How do you keep from becoming weary in doing good—and especially in doing good to people who are wearisome?

Throughout the Mediterranean world, a greeting between friends was usually marked by a kiss on each cheek. This was true as men greeted men and as women greeted women. Men, however, did not kiss women other than their wives, and women did not kiss men other than their husbands. To be holy meant to be God-like, to do things God's way rather than the way of the world. The purpose of a kiss was to show a sign of affection, respect, and affiliation. In the light of this explanation, read what the apostle Paul said to the Thessalonians:

Greet all of the brethren with a holy kiss (1 Thess. 5:25).

- How do you show affection, respect, and affiliation to others in your church?

- Are there people in your church that you know are uncomfortable with outward expressions of affection between believers? How do you greet or relate to those fellow believers?

• Why is it important for there to be a flow of genuine, holy affection within a body of believers?

The apostle Paul offered this closing prayer for the Thessalonians:

> We also pray always for you that our God would count you worthy of this calling, and fulfill all the good pleasure of His goodness and the work of faith with power, that the name of our Lord Jesus Christ may be glorified in you, and you in Him, according to the grace of our God and the Lord Jesus Christ (2 Thess. 1:11–12).

• What does it mean to be counted "worthy of this calling" to be a Christian?

• What does it mean to "fulfill all the good pleasure of His goodness"? To do the "work of faith with power"?

• Make a short list of people for whom you might pray this prayer on a regular basis.

I
Introspection and Implications

1. Is there someone in your life today who is unruly, fainthearted, or weak in faith? In what ways are you feeling challenged to respond to them or help them?

2. Evaluate your own praise, prayers, and expressions of thanksgiving. In what ways are you feeling challenged to pursue these aspects of communication with God that are definitely God's will for you?

3. Reflect on the ways you normally make choices and decisions. Do you ask the Holy Spirit for guidance? Do you consult God's Word?

4. Recall a time in your life when you heard something that you immediately knew was God's wisdom for your life. How did you respond? What was the result?

5. Think back to the last time someone lied to you or tempted you to join them in sin? How did you respond? What was the result?

C

Communicating the Good News

In what ways do you believe the practical Christian life described by Paul to the Thessalonians might be appealing to those who do not know Jesus as Savior?

In what ways are we to deal with sinners in:

• warning the unruly?

• confronting the fainthearted?

• upholding the weak?

• being patient with all?

How might these behaviors enhance an evangelistic presentation of the Gospel?

In what ways do we need to guard against making these behaviors a substitute for preaching the Gospel?

NOTES TO LEADERS
OF SMALL GROUPS

As the leader of a small discussion group, think of yourself as a facilitator with three main roles:

- Get the discussion started.

- Involve every person in the group.

- Encourage an open, candid discussion that remains Bible-focused.

You certainly don't need to be the person with all the answers! In truth, much of your role is to be a person who asks questions:

- What really impacted you most in this lesson?

- Was there a particular part of the lesson or a question that you found troubling?

- Was there a particular part of the lesson that you found encouraging or insightful?

- Was there a particular part of the lesson that you'd like to explore further?

Express to the group at the outset of your study that your goal as a group is to gain new insights into God's Word; this is not the forum for defending a point of doctrine or a theological opinion. Stay focused on what God's Word says and means. The purpose of the study is also to share insights on how to apply God's Word to everyday life. *Every* person in the group can and should contribute. The collective wisdom that flows from Bible-focused discussion is often very rich and deep.

Seek to create an environment in which every member of the group feels free to ask questions of other members in order to gain greater understanding. Encourage the group members to voice their appreciation to one another for new insights gained and be supportive of one another. Take the lead in this. Genuinely appreciate and value the contributions made by each person.

Since the letters of Paul are geared to our personal Christian lives as well as to the life of the church as a whole, you may experience a tendency in your group sessions to become overly critical of your *own* church or church leaders. Avoid the tendency to create discord or dissatisfaction. Don't use this Bible study as an opportunity to spread rumor, air anyone's dirty laundry, or criticize your pastor. Rather, seek positive ways to build up one another, including your church leaders. Seek positive outcomes and solutions to any problems you may identify.

You may want to begin each study by having one or more members of the group read through the section provided under "Bible Focus." Ask the group specifically if it desires to discuss any of the questions under the "Application" section, the "Supplemental Scriptures" section, and the "Implications" and "Communicating the Gospel" sections. You do not need to bring closure—or come to a definitive conclusion or consensus—about any one question asked in this study. Rather, if the group does not *have* a satisfactory Bible-based answer, encourage them to engage in further "asking, seeking, and knocking" strategies to discover the answers! Remember the words of Jesus: "Ask, and it will be given to you, seek, and you will find; knock, and it will be opened to you. For everyone who asks receives, and he who seeks finds, and to him who knocks it will be opened" (Matt. 7:7–8).

Finally, open and close your study with prayer. Ask the Holy Spirit, whom Jesus called the Spirit of Truth, to guide your discussion and to reveal what is of eternal benefit to you individually and as a group. As you close your study, ask the Holy Spirit to seal to your remembrance what you have read and studied and to show you in the upcoming days, weeks, and months *ways* to apply what you have studied to your daily life and relationships.

General Themes for the Lessons

Each lesson in this study has one or more core themes. Continually pull the group back to these themes. You can do this by asking simple questions, such as, "How does that relate to _____?" or "How does that help us better understand the concept of _____?" or "In what ways does that help us apply the principle of _____?"

A summary of general themes or concepts in each lesson is provided below:

Lesson #1
FAITHFUL AND EXEMPLARY BELIEVERS
Remaining faithful in times of affliction

Having the joy of the Holy Spirit

Receiving a preached or taught message as the Word of God

Applying the Word of God to practical daily life

Lesson #2
FRUITFUL AND TRUTHFUL MINISTERS
Exemplary ministry

Evaluating the lives of ministers

Honoring ministers

(Keep in mind that both professional clergy and lay persons are "ministers" of the Gospel)

Lesson #3
OVERCOMING SATAN'S HINDRANCES
Resisting the hindrances of satan

Overcoming obstacles to ministry

Remaining ardent in pursuing one's purpose and godly goals—in spite of difficulties or delays

Lesson #4
ABOUNDING MORE AND MORE
The process of sanctification

Godly aspiration

The perfecting of moral character

Lesson #5
READY FOR CHRIST'S COMING
The Second Coming

Being ready for Christ's coming

Remaining watchful and sober

Lesson #6

RESISTANCE TO APOSTASY

Apostasy

Patterns of sin that lead to resistance to the truth

Patterns of sin that lead to open rebellion against God

Lesson #7

ADMONITIONS AND BLESSINGS

The treatment of people with problems in the church

Knowing the will of God

Staying on God's path and avoiding detours into error

NOTES

NOTES

NOTES

NOTES

Printed in the USA
CPSIA information can be obtained
at www.ICGtesting.com
JSHW052122200424
61596JS00004B/12